The Official ChelseaFC Annual 2007

D0487582

A Grange Publication

© 2006. Published by Grange Communications Ltd., Edinburgh, under licence from Chelsea Football Club. Printed in the EU.

Photographs © Empics

ISBN 0 9550057 7 9

£6.99

Contents

Introduction

Welcome to the Official 2007 Chelsea Football Club Annual.

This year's edition is packed with more features, posters and quizzes than ever before as we look back on another fantastic season as well as looking forward to what could possibly be the greatest season in Chelsea's history!

New signings Andriy Shevchenko, Michael Ballack and Mikel John Obi are featured and every player is profiled so your favourite star will be in here somewhere! There's even a look at how Chelsea stars performed at the World Cup, plus a Junior Blues and Football Icon section.

When it comes to club annuals, this really is 'The Special One'!

That's Why We're Champions

August - Do Wah Didi

What better way to start the new campaign than with a trophy? As defending Premiership champions, Chelsea took on FA Cup holders Arsenal in the Community Shield at Cardiff's Millennium Stadium to kick off season 2005/06. The Blues were determined to start as they meant to go on and in an open and attractive game,

> "It was a tough game- a tight game - but under control from the start and when the game is under control, we know we can score goals."
> **Mourinho (v Spurs)**

Didier Drogba opened the scoring, after controlling a pass expertly on his chest and then volleying past Jens Lehman and he then added a second, showing his strength and poise to give his side breathing space. Cesc Fabregas pulled one back for the Gunners but despite their greater possession in the second half, the score remained 2-1 and the first piece of silverware was secured for José's boys.

The Premiership campaign began with a cracking match at Wigan, who were playing their first-ever game in the top-flight. Mourinho's warning that Wigan should not be underestimated was, as ever, spot-on as the hosts created several openings and struck the bar before the Blues showed their pedigree by snatching a last-minute winner in the shape of a Hernan Crespo scorcher. The goal fired a warning to the rest of the division that, even when their backs are to the wall, Chelsea's players are capable of grinding out victories.

Ghanaian international Michael Essien joined the Blues shortly after, following a protracted transfer deal that had lasted most of the summer and the fee of £244million was also a new club record. Other transfers included Tiago leaving for Lyon and Jiri Jarosik going out on loan to Birmingham for the season.

Arsenal were the first visitors to Stamford Bridge and Arsene Wenger's side were looking to avenge their Community Shield defeat two weeks earlier. Both sides created chances in the first half but there was to be only one goal scored and it was well worth waiting for – substitute Drogba got in behind the Gunners' defence but as he shaped to control the ball, it hit his knee and completely fooled the Arsenal keeper for a bizarre winner – not that the Chelsea fans were complaining! This was the first time the Blues had beaten Arsenal in the league for 10 years.

A comprehensive 4-0 win over West Brom followed three days later with Essien and Shaun Wright-Phillips making their full debuts. Two goals from Frank Lampard plus strikes from Joe Cole and Drogba put Chelsea top of the table. It was then off to White Hart Lane to face second-placed Tottenham who began brightly but later lost Egyptian striker Mido who was shown a straight red card for elbowing Asier Del Horno and it was Del Horno who opened the scoring 13 minutes later and a mis-hit Damien Duff volley made it 2-0 after the break to maintain an excellent start, which was continued with a 2-0 win at home to Sunderland with goals from Geremi and Drogba.

> **Lamps daddy of them all as Chelsea go top**
> THE INDEPENDENT

September - Maximum Points For Blues

With Arsenal and Manchester United dropping early points, Chelsea extended their lead at the top with a 2-0 win at Charlton Athletic thanks to goals from Crespo and Arjen Robben. Six points clear and the proud holders of a new

> **"I won't hold back. What I did last season was the consequence of something. So, if the competition is absolutely normal without anything strange, I would love to be a good boy and to behave well."**
> **- Mourinho**

clean-sheets record for the start of a season, the Blues were flying and the visit of Aston Villa held few fears but it was the Midlands who opened the scoring through Luke Moore. Within minutes, however, Lampard had levelled from a free kick and he added a second from the penalty spot after the break to secure a 2-1 win and a seventh consecutive league victory.

Wake up and smell the coffee - Chelsea are entertaining

THE OBSERVER

That's Why We're Champions

October - Lit By Lamps!

Having drawn 0-0 at Anfield in the Champions League just four days earlier, Chelsea returned for a Premiership clash with Liverpool believing – and claiming in the newspapers – that they now had the measure of Mourinho's

near the end to complete a resounding 4-1 win – Liverpool's biggest home defeat for 36 years and suddenly Anfield had gone very quiet!

Bolton were the next team to pay for having the temerity to take the lead at

Bottom of the table Everton were the side that ended the 100 per cent record as they battled out a 1-1 draw at Goodison Park. Beattie put the Merseysiders ahead from the spot but a Lampard special at least preserved Chelsea's unbeaten start to the campaign. There was a disappointment, however, in the Blues' first Carling Cup games of the season as Charlton triumphed 5-4 on penalties at the Bridge after the game had ended 1-1 after extra time.

> "Home or away, he can play in every system I want to play – he's what I call a player for every game. I wouldn't swap him for anyone." **Mourinho on Lampard**

men, the game had an added edge to it. The Blues began the game with an air of a team that wanted to prove a point and by the end of the afternoon Liverpool had been soundly thrashed in their own backyard. Drogba was felled for a penalty that Lampard tucked away but Stephen Gerrard levelled the scores soon after. Duff restored the lead before the break and Joe Cole added a third and Geremi added a killer fourth

the Bridge. Greek winger Stelios put them ahead with just four minutes gone, but two goals each from Drogba and Lampard plus a neat finish from Eidur Gudjohnsen meant Chelsea had equalled a club record of nine successive league wins. Things couldn't have begun any better and already people around the country were saying the title was as good as won – not that José Mourinho would allow such talk.

It was a case of normal service resuming with a 4-2 home victory over Blackburn – Drogba and Lampard gave the Blues a 2-0 lead before Craig Bellamy brought the scores level with two goals before half-time. Lampard's 100th career goal restored the lead and a deflected drive from Joe Cole sealed the points. All in all it had been a satisfying October.

> "Only lucky teams can beat us."
> - Jose Mourinho
> THE INDEPENDENT

November - We Don't Do 'Blips'

Lampard nets Player of the Month Award

BBC.CO.UK

It had to happen – though many wondered whether it might be possible for the Blues to remain unbeaten all season, the odds against such a feat were always stacked against them and the 1-0 defeat by Manchester United was seen by neutrals as keeping the Premiership title race alive for other clubs. Darren Fletcher's looping first half header was enough for United though José Mourinho remained upbeat after what was – coupled with the midweek loss at Real Betis – a second successive defeat. The

> "I don't believe in blips and besides, the teams behind can have blips."
> **Mourinho (v Man United)**

perfect remedy to the blip was a 3-0 home victory over Newcastle, which was achieved with goals from Cole, Crespo and Duff. Next up was an early evening trip to Fratton Park against a managerless Portsmouth side. Despite a bright opening, the hosts were eventually overwhelmed by goals from the in-form Crespo and Joe Cole – in fact, 2-0 rather flattered Portsmouth. That game was also Lampard's 160th consecutive Premiership start – a new record – having eclipsed the 159 made by David James.

December - Super Blues Unstoppable

John Terry's scrappy header against Middlesbrough proved to be the only goal of the game and kept the Blues' 100 per cent home record intact – and that scoreline was repeated a week later against Wigan Athletic with Terry again scoring the winner. The lead at the top was now 12 points and with Liverpool and Manchester United both continuing to win games there could be no let up.

A cross-London trip to Highbury - for the last time – also highlighted the 17-point gap between the clubs and by the end of the match that had increased to 20 points thanks to a first-half effort from Robben and a great individual effort from Joe Cole. Even though it was just coming up to Christmas, the general feeling was that Chelsea could only lose the title themselves having built up such a commanding lead at the top.

Fulham were the first team to score against Chelsea in eight games thanks to an uncharacteristic mistake by Cech, but even though they scored twice at the Bridge, they still lost 3-2 with goals from Robert Huth, Lampard and a wonderful volley from Crespo.

Wins over Manchester City and Birmingham completed a very happy Christmas period for the champions.

Chelsea can overcome Highbury hoodoo
THE INDEPENDENT

"We are very, very solid at the back and if there is a mistake, Petr Cech is there. The defenders work very hard and I'm very happy with the result."
Mourinho (v Arsenal)

That's Why We're Champions

January - Edging Closer...

> **"We have to concede goals again at some point, but at this moment, we are very, very solid at the back and if there is a mistake, Petr Cech is there. The defenders work very hard and I'm very happy with the result."**
> **Mourinho (v Arsenal)**

The Blues began 2006 with a 3-1 win at West Ham thanks to goals from Lampard, Crespo and Drogba and followed that up with a nervy 2-1 win over Huddersfield in the FA Cup 3rd Round. Carlton Cole's first start of the season saw the big striker open the scoring but the Yorkshire side equalised before Gudjohnsen's late winner. Maniche arrived on loan from Porto to add steel to a somewhat depleted midfield following Essien's injury and Geremi's absence due to the African Cup of Nations. Sunderland proved a tougher nut to crack than their bottom-of-the-table position suggested and took a shock lead at the Stadium of Light through Liam Lawrence but Crespo levelled before half-time and Robben's deflected shot was enough to clinch the points – though the Dutch winger was booked for the second time while celebrating and duly sent off.

Charlton again proved tricky opposition for their second visit to west London of the season and following Gudjohnsen's opener, Marcus Bent put the visitors level before Carvalho was sent off for a second bookable foul. Those would be the only two points dropped at home all season and with a healthy lead at the top, the Blues were still gunning for three trophies and they completed January with a 1-1 draw at Everton in the FA Cup 4th Round, Lampard's equaliser earning a replay at the Bridge.

Cole nets PFA Player of the Month Award

CHELSEAFC.COM

That's Why We're Champions

February - Arjen On Fire

Aston Villa were another team that belied their position and the Premiership clash at Villa Park saw the home side play their part in an entertaining 1-1 draw – Robben scoring for Chelsea. With no wins in three games, next up were Liverpool for the fourth meeting of the season – and once again the Merseyside outfit went home with nothing as goals from William Gallas and a cracker from Crespo securing a richly deserved 2-0 win. Progress to the last 16 of the FA Cup was confirmed in emphatic fashion with a 4-1 win over Everton in the FA Cup 4th Round with goals from Robben, Lampard, Crespo and Terry. Middlesbrough's 3-0 victory at the Riverside Stadium

> **"It's about winning silverware and we are not far from it. There are 17 matches to go and we need eight victories."**
> **Mourinho (v Liverpool)**

was the Blues' heaviest defeat of the season and with Manchester United continuing to win, the gap was down to 12 points at the top. A 3-1 win over

Colchester - already the fifth game of the month – meant the Blues were now in the last eight of the FA Cup, though the League One side were no pushovers, taking the lead and holding out until late on before two goals from Joe Cole won the day. A midweek Champions League defeat to Barcelona was tempered by a 2-0 victory over Portsmouth to edge the title ever closer. Lampard and Robben scored goals that increased the gap at the top to 15 points and was a pleasant way to end what had been a hectic month.

Mourinho weighs up Crespo's cunning against Drogba's power

THE GUARDIAN

March - Goodbye To The King

March began with the terrible news that Chelsea legend Peter Osgood had died suddenly aged 59. Floral tributes adorned the ground and supporters left shirts, flags and scarves at the Bridge in tribute to one of the club's greatest players.

The 2-1 win at West Brom was just the lift everybody needed at the club and goals from Cole and Drogba were enough to secure the victory, the players later dedicated the victory to the memory of Peter Osgood. Tottenham had no answer to Shaun Wright-Phillips' exciting forays forward and it was from his superb cross from the by-line that Michael Essien scored the opening goal. Spurs hit back with a goal on half-time through Jermain Jenas but it was William Gallas who had the last say with a fantastic shot in the last minute of the game sending Stamford Bridge wild. A controversial 1-0 defeat at Fulham saw Gallas see red for his part in a touchline brawl but John Terry's goal settled the FA Cup 6th Round clash with Newcastle. Manchester City were the next victims to leave the Bridge empty-handed, losing 2-0 thanks to two quick goals from Drogba.

"Drogba is sometimes a victim."
- José Mourinho

THE INDEPENDENT

"For me pressure is bird flu – I'm feeling a lot of pressure from the swan found in Scotland – it's not funny and I'm being serious. I'm more scared of the swan than football."
Mourinho on the lead being reduced to seven points

That's Why We're Champions

April - Make That A Double!

The Blues powered their way through April with five wins and a draw, beginning the month with a 0-0 draw at Birmingham City, allowing Manchester United to reduce the gap at the top to just seven points. West Ham led briefly at the Bridge and despite Maniche being sent off the Hammers were swept aside with goals from Drogba, Crespo, Terry and Gallas. With Manchester United dropping points at home to Sunderland, a win at Bolton would surely end the Reds' hopes once and for all and despite the home team's bright start goals from Terry and Lampard gave Chelsea a 2-0 win at the Reebok Stadium.

Lampard was on the scoresheet again in the 3-0 home win over Everton with Drogba and Essien completing the scoring. Fate conspired to pit the Blues yet again with Liverpool in the FA Cup semi-final for a fifth meeting of the season and an incredible 10th clash in the last two years! More than 30,000 Blues travelled to Old Trafford for the game but ultimately it wasn't to be Chelsea's day. Liverpool took an early lead through Riise and Terry had a goal ruled out before Luis Garcia made it 2-0. Drogba pulled one back but it wasn't enough and Liverpool moved on to the final against West Ham. Back to league action and

Chelsea would be crowned champions if they could beat their nearest rivals Manchester United at the Bridge – before, of course, they did. Gallas' header made it 1-0 and a tremendous individual effort by Joe Cole made it 2-0 and Carvalho scored to complete the rout.

The Blues were Premiership champions again and they'd done it in style, too! The celebrations went on long into the night and the Blues' home record was the best in more than a 100 years of league football.

It was also José Mourinho's fourth consecutive league title having won two at Porto prior to joining the Blues.

"It's done, it's over. Our second in a row and it's down to fantastic work from everybody. Consecutive championships for this club is a great achievement but we want more – I want more!"

Mourinho on securing a second title

May - After The Lord Mayor's Show

With the title in the bag a few first-team regulars were rested for the trip to Blackburn and despite a decent showing, the Blues lost 1-0 to a Robbie Savage free-kick. Newcastle also edged the spoils in the final game of the season at St James' Park with a goal 15 minutes from time from Titus Bramble. Successive defeats might not have been the envisaged end to the campaign most supporters had, but with the Premiership trophy safe and sound in the Stamford Bridge trophy room, the losses took nothing away from another fantastic season full of endeavour and style – after all, that's why we're champions!

Bramble's winner proves to be thorn in side

THE INDEPENDENT

"The league does not lie. We are 12 points clear and we have beaten Manchester United 3-0. This is our moment and we are going to enjoy it."
- **Frank Lampard**

Champions League

Maybe next time...

THINGS began brightly for the Blues who were looking to progress one stage further than the previous season's Champions League semi-final defeat to Liverpool, who had ironically been drawn in the same qualifying group this time around. With Anderlecht and Real Betis making up the group, confidence was high at the Bridge of making the knockout rounds.

Anderlecht were the first opponents and the Belgian side arrived in west London with a record number of successive Champions League defeats behind them - and a swerving free-kick from Lampard added yet another loss to their miserable run, though they came close to snatching a shock draw when they hit the post in the second half.

A trip to reigning Champions League holders Liverpool was next up for the battle of the Premiership clubs and with both teams creating few chances, a 0-0 draw was a fair result on the night. A 4-0 win over Real Betis - with goals from Drogba, Carvalho, Joe Cole and Crespo - meant that the Blues were halfway towards qualification for the next stage - at least it seemed that way. A surprise 1-0 loss - the Blues' first defeat of any kind all season - in the return game with Betis

meant the Blues had seven points from a possible 12 and still needed at least one more win from their remaining two games. Next up were Anderlecht, and this presented the perfect opportunity to all but seal a place in the last 32. The productive Lampard-Crespo understanding was responsible for Chelsea's opening goal with the Argentine forward volleying home from close range and Carvalho notched the second with an impressive finish from a corner - the 2-0 win meant the Blues couldn't be overhauled by third-placed Betis and were assured progression to the next stage with one game to play.

There was still much to play for in the final group game against Liverpool with the top-placed side likely to have easier opponents in the last 16. In a taut, tetchy affair, the Reds held on for a 0-0 draw and Chelsea's 'reward' was to be drawn against strongly fancied Barcelona for a place in the quarter-finals.

This was the game most people wanted for the final itself but one of Europe's two best teams had to bow out early - who would it be? Last season Chelsea had seen off Barca in dramatic fashion over two legs but

the Spaniards arrived for the first leg at the Bridge determined not to allow history to repeat itself. The Blues suffered the worst possible blow when Asier Del Horno's challenge on Lionel Messi was deemed a straight red card, and despite Messi's theatrics on the floor, the Blues were reduced to 10-men with plenty of time remaining. This was to be a pivotal moment in the tie and despite an own goal giving Chelsea the lead, John Terry's flick from a Ronaldinho free-kick also ended in his own net to level the scores. Worse was to follow as Barca made their numerical advantage pay with a late winner from Samuel Eto'o. The 2-1 defeat was the first 90-minute home loss under José Mourinho and also gave the Blues a mountainous task to reach the quarter-finals.

Ronaldinho's solo goal made the aggregate score 3-1 and virtually sealed the Blues' fate so Frank Lampard's last-minute penalty was no more than a consolation.

It was a disappointing end to the Champions League adventure, but 2007 could well be Chelsea's year, and don't despair!

Lethal Weapon
Andriy Shevchenko

ANDRIY SHEVCHENKO is known throughout Europe as the 'Lethal Weapon' and when you look at the Blues' new signing's goal-scoring record over the years, it's not hard to understand why! Regarded as a legend at his former club AC Milan, 'Sheva' is regarded as

> **"I am going from one big club to another and joining a team of champions."**
> **Andriy Shevchenko on Chelsea**

perhaps the best out-and-out striker in the world today – and now he is set to become one of the greatest strikers Chelsea has ever had.

Born in Dvirkivshchyna, Ukraine on September 29, 1976, Andriy was nine when the Chernobyl disaster occurred in 1986. His village, located not far from the nuclear plant, was also affected and his family was one among the thousands who had to abandon their homes and relocate to the coast to escape the after-effects.
Later that same year, Andriy, a talented junior

boxer, failed a dribbling test for entrance to a specialist sports school in Kyiv, but he did manage to impress a watching Dynamo Kiev scout while playing in a youth tournament, and so began his journey towards becoming the biggest star his country has ever produced.
His talents soon shone through and during an Under-14s tournament in Wales – the Ian Rush Cup, Andriy ended top scorer in the tournament, and was awarded a pair of Rush's boots as a prize by the Liverpool player himself.
He began his senior career with Kiev in 1994, making his debut as a teenager in the same year and though he played for his country on several occasions, it wasn't until 1998 when he scored a first-half hat-trick against Barcelona in the Nou Camp Stadium in a Champions League match that scouts around Europe really sat up and took notice.
A year later, and having won nine winners' medals with Kiev and scored 71 goals in 100 starts, AC Milan took him to Italy at a cost of $26m making his debut in August 1999. He soon settled into life with his new

club by becoming the first non-Italian to top the Serie A scoring charts in his first season.
Over the next two years, Andriy scored an incredible 51 goals in 89 games for Milan, despite the Italian giants failing to land any silverware during that time. In 2002/03, Milan won Serie A and the Champions League and in doing so Andriy became the first Ukrainian to land a winners' medal in Europe's premier tournament.
He then picked up the European Footballer of the Year award in 2004 and was also named by Pele as one of the 125 greatest living footballers.
The Milan fans adored Andriy and his 173 goals made him the second top scorer in the club's history, but despite the record being within his grasp, the lure of Chelsea proved too great and shortly before leading his country to their first ever appearance in a World Cup, he signed a four-year deal with the Blues saying, "I am going from one big club to another and joining a team of champions."
At last, José Mourinho – who described the signing as a "dream that had become a reality" – has got his man. Now watch the Lethal Weapon – fully locked and loaded – go!

BIGCFCQUIZ2007

With three points for each correct answer, can you top Chelsea's points total for season 2005/06? Your target is 92 and if you can't top that, the Chelsea board expects you to qualify for Champions League football… or you could be out! You might need a little help with the historical questions so make sure you've got a good team behind you!

1. Who won Chelsea's Young Player of the Year award for 2006?

2. Who was the first Chelsea player to score at the World Cup?

3. Which country does Chelsea chairman Bruce Buck come from?

4. What kind of animal is on the Chelsea club crest?

5. Which club did former chairman Ken Bates eventually move to?

6. How many times did Gianfranco Zola win the club's Player of the Year award?

7. Which current Chelsea star won a gold medal at the 2000 Olympics?

8. Which Chelsea player was born in Florida?

9. Which position did José Mourinho's father Felix play in?

10. Which country does assistant-manager Baltemar Brito come from?

11. Chelsea were the first English football team to travel by aeroplane to an away match – true or false?

12. How many points did Chelsea

have at the end of the 2004/05 season?

13. Name three clubs Shaun Wright-Phillips' dad, Ian Wright played for (one point for each)

14. Which game was Carlo Cudicini named captain for last season?

15. John Terry spent a short time on loan with which club?

16. Which club was Jiri Jarosik sold to?

17. Name the goalkeeper who joined Millwall in 2006?

18. Can you name the Manchester City player sent off at Stamford Bridge last season?

19. Andriy Shevchenko spent a brief loan spell with Barcelona prior to joining Chelsea – true or false?

20. Which year was Chelsea FC first founded?

21. What is Joe Cole's middle name?

22. Can you name the Premiership manager and former England defender who has a daughter named Chelsea?

23. Who is Chelsea's Head of Development and Scouting?

24. Who did Chelsea beat in 1971 to win the European Cup Winners' Cup?

25. Which legendary Chelsea striker scored five goals in one match on three separate occasions?

26. Can you name the club's all-time leading goal scorer?

27. Who was the Chelsea boss before José Mourinho arrived?

28. Who was known as 'The King of Stamford Bridge'?

29. Which current Chelsea player has played more than 50 times for Ireland?

30. True or false: Geremi used to play for Real Madrid?

31. Chelsea's biggest Premiership win in 2005/06 was against which club?

32. How many times did the Blues play Liverpool last season?

33. Which club did Gianfranco Zola sign from in 1996?

34. Which number shirt does Michael Ballack play in for Germany?

35. Who is Chelsea's Chief Executive?

36. Who won the Samsung Players' Player of the Year for 2006?

37. Can you name the four Chelsea players who were voted in the PFA Premiership team of 2005/06?

38. How many times has Chelsea won the Premiership?

PREMIERSHIP TABLE 2005/2006

01	Chelsea	38	91
02	Manchester United	38	83
03	Liverpool	38	82
04	Arsenal	38	67
05	Tottenham Hotspur	38	65
06	Blackburn Rovers	38	63
07	Newcastle United	38	58
08	Bolton Wanderers	38	56
09	West Ham United	38	55
10	Wigan Athletic	38	51
11	Everton	38	50
12	Fulham	38	48
13	Charlton Athletic	38	47
14	Middlesbrough	38	45
15	Manchester City	38	43
16	Aston Villa	38	42
17	Portsmouth	38	38
18	Birmingham City	38	34
19	West Bromwich Albion	38	30
20	Sunderland	38	15

Answers on page 60/61

WhoSaidThis...?

1 "I'm still a young kid, I still need to grow. I'm still growing. I'm nearly 6 feet 3 inches."

2 "When I was younger I thought about going to play in the sun, but then it became clear the Premiership was the place to be."

3 "Football is most technical in Spain and most physical in England. In Italy it is a mix of everything so I am prepared for everything. I am happy to face the new challenge."

4 "I want to enjoy and be in the team where I can be a better player and I want to reach the top. I will play where I am put and I am going to do my best."

5 "Every experience I have had here has been very special. I am at the biggest club in the world and that is very good for me. I want to stay here. I want to win even more."

6 "José Mourinho instils a winning mentality in you at Chelsea and we are bringing that into the England squad. You can see the confidence of the Chelsea boys around the place."

7 "You always learn. I learn in every training, every game, and those experiences you always try to take with you, and develop as a player. I think people forget sometimes I'm only 22 still, I'm still learning and developing."

8 "Unfortunately in the emotion of winning the game my comments have come across partly in the wrong way. I want to make clear that I don't dive, this was the intention of my answer."

9 "We don't lose a lot of matches. But when it happens you can't do anything. When the game is finished, you have to move on."

10 "You have to have a strong mentality to succeed and playing at Chelsea has given me this. I am not afraid of anyone."

Answers on page 60/61

CHELSEA FC
STADIUM TOURS & MUSEUM

VISIT STAMFORD BRIDGE AND GO BEHIND-THE-SCENES INTO AREAS OF CHELSEA FOOTBALL CLUB THAT YOU WOULD ONLY HAVE EVER DREAMED OF SEEING!

Your fully guided tour will take you into the Home Dressing Room, the Press Room, the Players Tunnel, the Managers Dug-out and the Centenary Museum. You can even have your photograph taken with the Barclays Premiership Trophy!

The tours are suitable for fans of all ages and run throughout the year so do not miss this once-in-a-lifetime opportunity and book your tickets now!

All Tours and photo opportunities with the Barclays Premiership Trophy are subject to availability, alteration or cancellation without prior notice. Stadium Tours and Museum will be closed on all home Matchdays.

ORDER ON-LINE ON AT
WWW.CHELSEAFC.COM/TOURS
OR CALL 0870 603 0005

You're Indestructible

Joe Cole

THERE was a time, not so long ago, when it seemed Joe Cole might be on his way out of Stamford Bridge. Nobody could question his fantastic skill and trickery, but when José Mourinho threatened to drop him after one particular game stating that he was playing for himself and not the team, Joe's career took a new direction.

Shocked at his manager's views and knowing that he needed to tweak certain parts of his game or end up in the reserves, Joe listened and thought about what he needed to do to ensure he became an indispensable first-team player.

From that moment on, he became perhaps Chelsea's most improved player and the knock-on benefits also saw him become an England regular. In short, he listened, worked hard and

He won his first England cap aged 19 and things couldn't have been going better for the youngster

with a new lucrative contract signed this summer, he is now reaping the benefits.

His road to stardom began on November 8, 1981 when Joeseph John Cole was born in Archway, London, though he was raised in Camden. It wasn't so long into his school years that people realised he had a special talent and was considered a child prodigy and attracted national media coverage for his skills as a young boy.

Snapped up by West Ham, he glided through the Hammers' academy and at the age of 16, Manchester United were reportedly willing to pay £10million for him! The interest was not encouraged and a year later Joe made his league debut – ironically, against Manchester United – and within just four years he was the club captain at Upton Park.

He won his first England cap aged 19 and things couldn't have been going better for the youngster. But when Harry Redknapp left West Ham, one of the country's most exciting midfielder's progress suddenly seemed to stall and some even wondered if he'd reached his peak too soon.

Thankfully, in 2003, Claudio Ranieri paid £6.6million to bring Joe to Chelsea but having left a club where he was guaranteed first-team football, he found it tough to tie down a place in the starting line-up at the Bridge. It seemed there was an endless array of talented midfielders joining the Blues and Joe played sporadically here and there and this continued when Mourinho took over in 2004.

Then, despite scoring the winner against Liverpool, the Chelsea boss criticised Joe for neglecting his defensive duties and it seemed his days with the club might be numbered – but Joe proved that by listening to advice and working hard in training, it's possible to turn things around and when injuries presented him with a sustained run in the team, he grasped the opportunity with both hands. Joe proved to his manager that the Chelsea team was better with him in it and has never looked back since.

Last season, 24-year-old Joe was outstanding and scored many spectacular goals with his work rate as impressive as his range of skill and tricks. He was a regular for his country in the World Cup in Germany and with more than 30 caps under his belt already, he is set to become a permanent fixture for both club and country for many years to come.

SimplyTheBest

Chelsea FC asked supporters to vote for their favourite ever 11 players to mark the 2005 Centenary year. Thousands of Blues' fans sent in their all-time teams and below are the results – the Chelsea dream team!

Peter Bonetti

Steve Clarke

John Terry

Marcel Desailly

Graeme Le Saux

Charlie Cooke

Frank Lampard

Dennis Wise

Gianfranco Zola

Peter Osgood

Bobby Tambling

Peter Bonetti
1959-1979
Apps: 600
Goals: 0

John Terry
1997-present
Apps: 259 (+19 sub)
Goals: 30

Frank Lampard
2001-present
Apps: 270 (+15 sub)
Goals: 69

Peter Osgood
1964-1974
Apps: 380
Goals: 150

Steve Clarke
1987-1998
Apps: 321 (+9 sub)
Goals: 7

Marcel Desailly
1998-2004
Apps: 214 (+3 sub)
Goals: 7

Charlie Cooke
1966-1972 & 1974-1978
Apps: 289 (+10 sub)
Goals: 22

Bobby Tambling
1958-1970
Apps: 370
Goals: 202

Graeme Le Saux
1987-1993 & 1997-2003
Apps: 280 (+ 32 sub)
Goals: 16

Dennis Wise
1990-2001
Apps: 434 (+11 sub)
Goals: 74

Gianfranco Zola
1996-2003
Apps: 260 (+52 sub)
Goals: 80

SpotTheBall

Answers on page 60/61

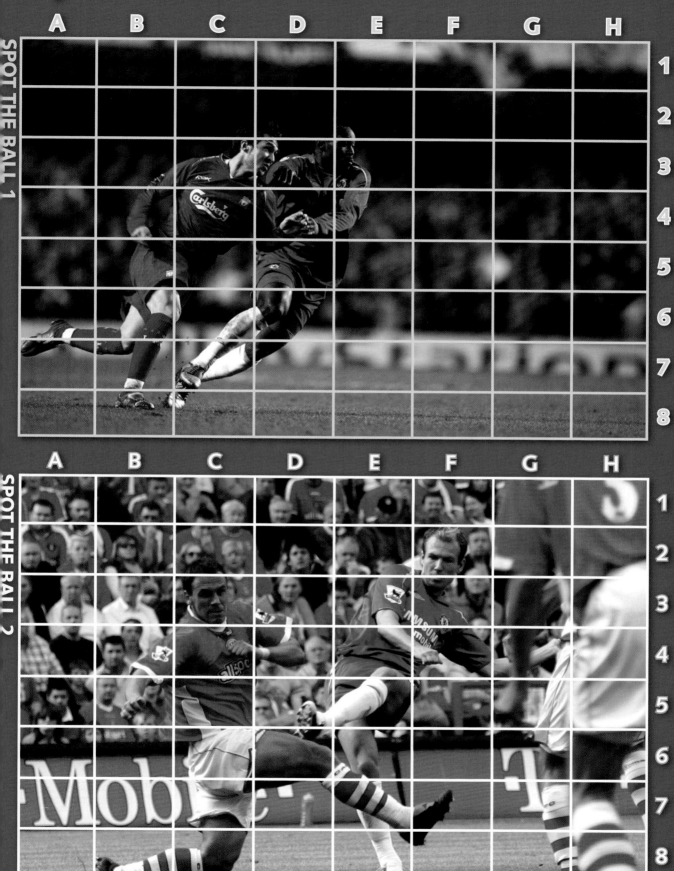

SPOT THE BALL 1

SPOT THE BALL 2

FrankLampard

Ballack&Blue
Michael Ballack

MICHAEL BALLACK became a Chelsea player shortly after the 2005/06 season ended and for José Mourinho, it ended a lengthy chase for the highly-rated Germany skipper. The powerhouse midfielder is set to become a key part of the Blues' attempt to land the Champions League trophy in 2007 and his all-action style and versatility mean he is perfectly equipped to have a major impact in the Premiership. Signed on a free transfer from Bayern Munich, Ballack began his career as a youth with BSG Motor and joined them aged just seven. During his third season with the junior side he scored 57 goals in 16 games and soon moved to Chemintzer FC and in 1995 he won his first professional contract and soon earned the nickname 'Little Kaiser' in reference to the great Franz Beckenbauer. Though his new club were relegated that season, he made his debut for the Germany Under-21s as his career continued to blossom. He remained with Chemintzer as they attempted to win their place back in the second division, but despite playing every game and scoring 10 goals, they narrowly missed out on promotion. FC Kaiserslautern, who had been promoted back to the Bundesliga (top division), gave Ballack the chance to play on a much bigger stage, which he gratefully accepted.

The move proved to be inspired for both player and club, as Kaiserslautern became the first newly promoted team to win the Bundesliga with Ballack making a strong impact following his full debut against Bayer Leverkusen. He made his first appearance for the German national team in May 1999 and two months later joined Leverkusen for a fee in the region of £3million. He was an instant success for his new club and they seemed set to become Bundesliga champions in his first season when they needed just a point against struggling SpVgg Unterhaching – but Ballack scored a stunning own goal and they missed out! To many, it at least proved that the rising star was only human after all.

During the 2001/02 season, Ballack had three gut-wrenching near misses for both club and country – first Leverkusen narrowly missed winning the title and lost the Champions League Final, then Germany lost the World Cup Final in 2002 – at least he could take solace from being voted German Footballer of the Year – his first of three such awards. He moved on to Bayern Munich for approximately £8million where he became a huge crowd favourite, helping his new side to the league title while becoming an integral member of the national team. In three amazing years with Bayern he won three league and German Cup doubles and also became captain of both his club and country. With a desire to try his hand in another country and despite interest from Real Madrid, AC Milan and Manchester United, Ballack finally opted for a move to Chelsea and signed a three-year deal prior to the 2006 World Cup. He said: "I asked some players about England - Robert Huth, Jens Lehmann - and they told me good things about this country and I am happy to be here." Now the father-of-three aims to help the Blues to Champions League glory – one of the few winners' medals missing from his personal collection.

> **I asked some players about England - Robert Huth, Jens Lehmann - and they told me good things about this country and I am happy to be here**

I WAITED 50 YEARS THEN TWO CAME TOGETHER !

WorldCupBlues

With no less than 16 players, Chelsea were the Premiership's most represented team at the 2006 World Cup Finals in Germany – here is how the Blues' stars fared in Germany…

Wayne Bridge - England
Pld: 0 Gls: 0 Assists: 0

A disappointing tournament for Wayne who spent much of last season with Fulham. The form of Ashley Cole meant there was no opportunity for him to play and he was the only Chelsea star not to take any part in competitive games.

Didier Drogba - Ivory Coast
Pld: 2 Gls: 1 Assists: 0

Didier's Ivory Coast side put up a brave performance in a very tough qualifying group that included Holland and Argentina. His 82nd minute goal against Argentina was his first in the finals but Ivory Coast failed to progress past the first stage.

Paulo Ferreira - Portugal
Pld: 3 Gls: 0 Assists: 0

Paulo played half of Portugal's games as his country reached the semi-finals. He was solid and effective when called upon by Luiz Felipe Scolari and was unlucky not to play more games.

Petr Cech - Czech Republic
Pld: 3 Gls: 0 Assists: 0

Petr Cech would have been expecting to play more than just the group stages after the Czech Republic won their first game 3-0 against the USA, but Ghana and Italy both beat them 2-0 and eliminated the Czechs from the tournament. Petr's performance against Ghana was almost superhuman and but for him, Ghana would have won by many more goals.

Michael Essien - Ghana
Pld: 3 Gls: 0 Assists: 0

Michael Essien enjoyed a good World Cup with Ghana qualifying for the knockout stages on their first appearance at the Finals. Essien picked up two yellow cards and missed the Round of 16 against Brazil and Ghana were beaten 3-0, but his country celebrated what was a fantastic achievement and Essien's quality shone throughout.

Arjen Robben - Holland
Pld: 3 Gls: 1 Assists: 1

Arjen Robben's wing wizardry for the Dutch couldn't prevent them making a surprise exit at the hands of Portugal in the Round of 16. Robben was a constant thorn to the opposition's defences and he created one goal and scored another before the former Blues' midfielder Maniche dumped Holland out.

Hernan Crespo - Argentina
Pld: 4 Gls: 3 Assists: 1

Argentina were expected to reach and win the World Cup Final after their group matches, so impressive were the South Americans. Hernan Crespo would surely have been a contender for top tournament scorer if they had gone all the way, but they lost to Germany on penalties in the quarter-finals. Crespo scored goals against Serbia, Ivory Coast and Mexico but was rested for the clash with Holland.

Michael Ballack - Germany
Pld: 5 Gls: 0 Assists: 1

German skipper Michael Ballack couldn't hide his disappointment at not being able to lift the World Cup on home soil. But Ballack had an excellent tournament and almost inspired his team to a famous win. His intelligent, energetic midfield performances will be a huge asset to the Blues this season and third place at the World Cup is something to be proud of.

Robert Huth - Germany
Pld: 1 Gls: 0 Assists: 0

Robert Huth made just one appearance for Germany during a 3-0 win over Ecuador. The young centre-back was named in every squad but was an unused sub in six matches.

Andriy Shevchenko - Ukraine
Pld: 5 Gls: 2 Assists: 1

Andriy Shevchenko enjoyed his first World Cup as Ukraine surpassed all expectations by reaching the last eight. Things couldn't have begun worse for 'Sheva' when Spain beat them 4-0 in their opening game but they stuck to their task with great pride to beat Tunisia and Saudi Arabia to set up a last 16 match with Switzerland. After a drab match, the game went to penalties and Sheva's jinx struck again as he missed from the spot, but Ukraine still progressed to the last eight where they were well beaten by Italy. At least Andriy bagged two goals (against Tunisia and Saudi Arabia) and appeared to enjoy every minute of his time in Germany.

Frank Lampard - England
Pld: 5 Gls: 0 Assists: 0

By his own high standards, Frank Lampard didn't enjoy the most productive of tournaments. Looking tired and not his prolific best, Lamps missed chances he'd gobble up every week in the Premiership and his stats of no goals and no assists prove the point. He was devastated to miss a penalty in the shoot-out with Portugal but he'll be back to his best and will be a key member of Steve McClaren's new England team.

John Terry - England
Pld: 5 Gls: 0 Assists: 0

Blues' skipper John Terry tried his best to help England to the World Cup Final but ultimately too many players had a poor tournament. Terry typifies the

English fighting spirit and it's doubtful he could have done any more personally and it's such attributes that now make him a possible captain for his country following Beckham's decision to step down.

Joe Cole - England
Pld: 5 Gls: 1 Assists: 1
Joe Cole was one of England's better performers in Germany, but even his skills couldn't prevent defeat to the Portuguese. The talented Blues' star did at least score one of the best goals of the competition, volleying home an incredible shot against Sweden. He will enjoy success with his country in future years, no doubt about it!

Ricardo Carvalho - Portugal
Pld: 6 Gls: 0 Assists: 0
Portugal almost made it to the World Cup final and Ricardo Carvalho's performances throughout were one of the main reasons. A defensive rock, he was one of the players of the tournament and who could forget his involvement in helping England's exit? It was Ricardo's challenge on Wayne Rooney that resulted in the England striker's foul that led to him being sent off – though it was hardly Carvalho's fault as he lay in agony on the turf!

Claude Makelele - France
Pld: 7 Gls: 0 Assists: 0
It was a case of so near yet so far for Claude Makelele. The diminutive Chelsea midfielder was at the heart of France's push to the World Cup final and he was never less than excellent throughout. Claude seemed to enjoy a more attacking role with the French and he can be proud of his exploits in what will likely be his last World Cup.

William Gallas - France
Pld: 7 Gls: 0 Assists: 0
Like Makelele, Gallas was a rock for the French in all the games he played. Solid at the back and a constant threat from set-pieces, Gallas' partnership with Lillian Thuram at the heart of Les Blues' back four was one of the best in the tournament. He should be proud of his considerable achievements in Germany.

Super Eagle
Finally Lands
Mikel John Obi

NIGERIAN teenager Mikel John Obi arrived at Stamford Bridge in the summer with his long wait to sign for the Blues brought to an end. Chelsea reached agreement with both Manchester United and Norwegian club Lyn Oslo to bring the exciting youngster to west London and rescue him from the limbo he found himself in for the last year.

The talented central midfielder was born John Michael Nchekube Obi in Plateau State, Nigeria on April 22, 1987 The son of a former civil servant, Mikel played youth football for Plateau United and Ajax Cape Town and starred in the FIFA Under-17 World Championships in Finland in 2003.

Two years later, he was again grabbing the headlines for his impressive displays as Nigeria reached the World Youth Championship final, only to lose 2-1 to Argentina. Curiously, when commentators continually mispronounced his middle name Michael as 'Mikel' he decided he liked the incorrect version so much he decided to keep it!

A glittering career now lies ahead of him and, for many in his homeland, he is seen as the future of Nigerian football. The youngest member of the Chelsea first team squad, Mikel's arrival delighted José Mourinho who said: "Everybody was in love, not just me, but the players who were amazed at such a young boy coming from nowhere and training with us with such quality.

"You saw him in the African Cup of Nations, playing like a giant in the middle of players like Okocha, Yobo, Drogba and Eto'o at an absolutely unbelievable level.

"He's a midfield player, we can teach him to be more complete, to defend better and to get more intensity in the game. He's bright in the way he thinks football, technically he's fantastic and it's just a point to get the intensity of the English game."

Now Chelsea fans will be keen to catch a glimpse of a player who literally has the world at his feet – and at 6ft 3in, you can't really miss

> ## "You saw him in the African Cup of Nations, playing like a giant in the middle of players like Okocha, Yobo, Drogba and Eto'o at an absolutely unbelieveable level."
> ## Mourinho on Mikel John Obi

him, especially as he claims he is still growing!

"Everybody's got his style of play," says Mikel. "I'm a midfield player who just wants to go in there and do my stuff. I'm not a defensive player, I like making the team play, get into the game, keep moving around, keeping looking for the ball and make sure the team plays well."

NameGame

Can you work out the Chelsea players
from the anagrams below?

1 – ME HISS NICE ALE _____

2 – HI LAMB CAKE CALL _____

3 – DRINK HEAVY HE CONS _____

4 – DO HORN REALISE _____

5 – HIM LIKE NO JOB _____

6 – U ALSO LOOK MAN _____

7 – ALS RAID AS A RAN _____

8 – THY NOT RANG AN _____

9 – BEAK MAY V MY LAMAS _____

10 – EEJ COOL _____

Answers on page 60/61

Quiz Detective

Can you work out the Chelsea players from the pictures below?

Answers on page 60/61

PlayerProfiles

PETR CECH ▶

Squad Number: 1
Position: Goalkeeper
Date of Birth: May 20, 1982
Birthplace: Plzen,
Czech Republic
Height: 6 5
Signed: July 1, 2004
Fee: £7m
Previous Clubs: Chmel
Blsany, Sparta Prague, Rennes

◀ CARLO CUDICINI

Squad Number: 23
Position: Goalkeeper
Date of Birth: Sept 6, 1973
Birthplace: Milan, Italy
Height: 6 1
Signed: July 20, 1999
Fee: £160,000
Previous Clubs: Milan,
Lazio, Prato, Castel di Sangro

HENRIQUE HILARIO ▶

Squad Number: 40
Position: Goalkeeper
Date of Birth: Oct 21, 1975
Birthplace: Sao Pedro da Cova, Portugal
Height: 6 2
Signed: July 1, 2006
Fee: £0
Previous Clubs: Nacional,
Academica de Coimbra, FC Porto

RICARDO CARVALHO

Squad Number: 6
Position: Central Defender
Date of Birth: May 18, 1978
Birthplace: Amarante,
Portugal
Height: 6
Signed: July 27, 2004
Fee: £19.85m
Previous Clubs: Porto

WAYNE BRIDGE

Squad Number: 18
Position: Full-back
Date of Birth: Aug 5, 1980
Birthplace: Southampton,
England
Height: 5 10
Signed: Jan 19, 2006
Fee: £7m
Previous Clubs:
Southampton, Fulham (loan)

PAULO FERREIRA ▶

Squad Number: 20
Position: Full-back
Date of Birth: Jan 18, 1979
Birthplace: Cascais, Portugal
Height: 5 11
Signed: July 1, 2004
Fee: £13.2m
Previous Clubs: Porto

PlayerProfiles

WILLIAM GALLAS ▶

Squad Number: 3
Position: Central Defender
Date of Birth: Aug 17, 1977
Birthplace: Asnieres, France
Height: 6 0
Signed: May 18, 2001
Fee: £6.2m
Previous Clubs: Caen,
Marseille

◀ JOHN TERRY

Squad Number: 26
Position: Central Defender
Date of Birth: Dec 7, 1980
Birthplace: London, England
Height: 6 1
Signed: Trainee
Fee: £0
Previous Clubs:
Nottingham Forest (loan)

KHALID BOULAHROUZ ▶

Squad Number: 9
Position: Defender
Date of Birth: Dec 28, 1981
Birthplace: Maassluis, Holland
Height: 6
Signed: Aug 22, 2006
Fee: Undisclosed
Previous Clubs: RKC Waalwijk,
SV Hamburg

JOE COLE ▶

Squad Number: 10
Position: Midfield
Date of Birth: Nov 8, 1981
Birthplace: London, England
Height: 5 9
Signed: Aug 6, 2003
Fee: £6.6m
Previous Clubs: West Ham

LASSANA DIARRA ▶

Squad Number: 19
Position: Midfield
Date of Birth: Mar 10, 1985
Birthplace: Paris, France
Height: 5 8
Signed: July 15, 2005
Fee: £0
Previous Clubs: Le Havre

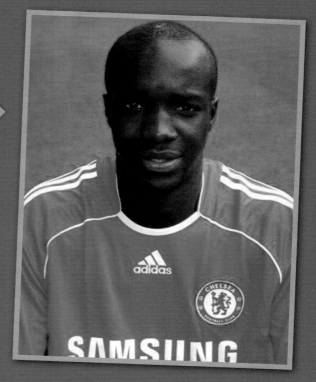

MICHAEL ESSIEN

Squad Number: 5
Position: Midfield
Date of Birth: Dec 3, 1982
Birthplace: Accra, Ghana
Height: 6 0
Signed: Aug 19, 2005
Fee: £24.4m
Previous Clubs: Bastia, Lyon

GEREMI

Squad Number: 14
Position: Midfield
Date of Birth: Dec 20, 1978
Birthplace: Batousam, Cameroon
Height: 5 9
Signed: July 16, 2003
Fee: £6.9m
Previous Clubs: Real Madrid, Middlesbrough (loan)

FRANK LAMPARD

Squad Number: 8
Position: Midfield
Date of Birth: June 20, 1978
Birthplace: Romford, England
Height: 6 0
Signed: June 15, 2001
Fee: £11m
Previous Clubs: West Ham

CLAUDE MAKELELE ▶

Squad Number: 4
Position: Midfield
Date of Birth: Feb 18, 1973
Birthplace: Kinshasa, DR Congo
Height: 5 7
Signed: Aug 31, 2003
Fee: £13.9m
Previous Clubs: Real Madrid

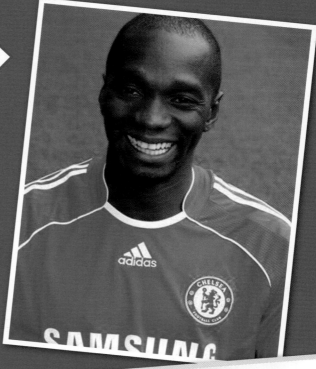

▶ SHAUN WRIGHT-PHILLIPS

Squad Number: 24
Position: Midfield
Date of Birth: Oct 25, 1981
Birthplace: London, England
Height: 5 6
Signed: July 18, 2005
Fee: £21m
Previous Clubs: Manchester City

◀ ARJEN ROBBEN

Squad Number: 16
Position: Midfield
Date of Birth: Jan 23, 1984
Birthplace: Bedum, Netherlands
Height: 5 11
Signed: July 1, 2004
Fee: £12m
Previous Clubs: FC Groningen, PSV Eindhoven

PlayerProfiles

MICHAEL BALLACK ▶

Squad Number: 13
Date of Birth: Sept 26, 1976
Birthplace: Chemintz, Germany
Height: 6 3
Signed: May 15, 2006
Fee: £0
Previous Clubs: FC Chemintz, Kaiserslautern, Bayer Leverkusen, Bayern Munich

◀ MIKEL JOHN OBI

Squad Number: 12
Date of Birth: Apr 22, 1987
Birthplace: Plateau State, Nigeria
Height: 5 11
Signed: June 3, 2006
Fee: £16m
Previous Clubs: Lyn

DIDIER DROGBA ▶

Squad Number: 11
Date of Birth: Mar 11, 1978
Birthplace: Abidjan, Ivory Coast
Height: 6 2
Signed: July 20, 2004
Fee: £24m
Previous Clubs: Le Mans, Guingamp, Marseille

SALOMON KALOU ▶

Squad Number: 21
Date of Birth: Aug 5, 1985
Birthplace: Oume, Ivory Coast
Height: 6
Signed: May 30, 2006
Fee: Undisclosed
Previous Clubs: Feyenoord, Excelsior (loan)

◀ ANDRIY SHEVCHENKO

Squad Number: 7
Date of Birth: Sept 29, 1976
Birthplace: Dvirkivshchyna, Ukraine
Height: 6 0
Signed: May 31, 2006
Fee: Undisclosed
Previous Clubs: Dynamo Kiev, AC Milan

SHOW YOUR TRUE COLOURS

SHOW YOUR TRUE COLOURS, BE A TRUE BLUE.

Being a Chelsea fan is all well and good, but becoming a member of True Blue is something else. True Blue is the official Chelsea membership scheme and as a member you'll get a fantastic package of goodies and benefits, especially created for junior Chelsea supporters. Benefits include members' match tickets cheaper than those on General Sale, an exclusive members' pack including a Chelsea scarf, DVD (for over 5s), Chelsea flag, wallchart and other goodies plus a fabulous Bridge Kids quarterly magazine.

All from just £15 a year for kids. And why not get Mum and Dad to join as well, there is a separate scheme available for adults, priced at just £42.

To join, visit **www.chelseafc.com** and click on **'True Blue'**.

WWW. CHELSEAFC.COM

DidierDrogba

Crossword

ACROSS

1   The King of Stamford Bridge (5,6)
4   Cameroonian midfielder (6)
5   Soccer AMs Chelsea supporting presenter (3,7)
7   José's first club as manager (7)
9   Who knocked the Blues out of the Champions League? (9)
13   Team who inflicted Chelsea's biggest defeat last season (13)
17   Andriy Shevchenko's nickname in Italy (6,6)
18   Name of Shaun Wright-Phillips' younger brother (7)
19   Young striker who joined from Feyenoord (7, 5)

DOWN

2   Ukrainian striker's squad number (5)
3   Country Michael Ballack captains (7)
5   Frank Lampard scored this many goals last season (6)
6   Goalkeeper who went on loan to Watford (4,2,8)
8   Player with most starts last season (4,5)
10   Only player to be sent off twice in 2006/06 (5,6)
11   Argentine striker (6,6)
12   Winner of Football Icon I (3,7)
14   2006/07 Community Shield opponents (8)
15   Biggest seating area at Stamford Bridge (4,5)
16   Country of Mikel John Obi (7)

1 Joe Cole v Manchester United
29/04/06

Like Frank Lampard, Joe Cole only seems to score spectacular goals and this strike against Manchester United was, even by his standards, a bit special. Collecting Drogba's flick, Cole controlled the ball before taking on three United defenders. With superb trickery he wriggled away from all three leaving him clear on goal and he finished emphatically with a powerful drive past Edwin van der Sar.

2 Hernan Crespo v Liverpool
05/02/06

Having had one effort ruled out for offside, Crespo seemed determined to score the goal his all-round play had merited. He challenged a ball into the Liverpool box but when it was cleared, he remained alert to Asier Del Horno's clever lob and raced behind the defence to lash home a left-foot drive from the corner of the box.

3 William Gallas v Spurs
11/03/06

With the scores locked at 1-1 and the referee glancing at his watch, William Gallas picked the ball up on the left and headed for the Spurs box – he checked back inside, evaded another challenge before letting rip with an unstoppable drive past Paul Robinson to win the game in spectacular fashion.

4 Hernan Crespo v Wigan Athletic
14/08/05

With Wigan pressing for a winning goal with just 30 seconds left, the ball was cleared back into the hosts' half where Didier Drogba headed on to Hernan Crespo. The Argentine striker controlled the ball, turned and made room for a left-foot curling drive that gave the keeper no chance and won the game for the Blues.

5 Arjen Robben v Charlton
17/09/05

Chelsea led 1-0 at The Valley thanks to Crespo's soaring header and were looking to tie the game up when Duff picked the ball up on the right of the Charlton box. He laid a pass back to Robben who controlled the ball and, encouraged by the lack of attention, moved into the box, shimmied left and then curled a perfect shot into the top left-hand corner. A peach of a goal!

6 Hernan Crespo v Real Betis
19/10/05

Frank Lampard played a wonderful ball from his own half out to Shaun Wright-Phillips, who raced with a Betis defender to get in a wicked first-time cross. Meeting the ball full on was Crespo to bullet his header past the Spanish keeper and make the score 4-0 on the night – a terrific team goal that took just eight seconds to create.

7 Frank Lampard v Everton
23/10/05

Lamps rarely scores tap-ins or scruffy goals and his reputation for long-range scorchers was enhanced in a scrappy match at Everton. Picking up Asier Del Horno's throw-in 30 yards out Lampard fired in a swerving shot that flew past the keeper and into the back of the net like an exocet missile.

8 Didier Drogba v West Ham
02/01/06

Eidur Gudjohnsen's perfect long ball into the path of Didier Drogba meant that the Ivory Coast star had only to control the ball well to give himself a chance on goal. He took one touch and then from a difficult angle sent a cracking low drive past Roy Carroll to complete a 3-1 victory at Upton Park.

9 Joe Cole v Colchester
19/02/06

Having just put the Blues 2-1 up against a stubborn Colchester side, Joe Cole ran with the ball towards goal. With several defenders still ahead of him he shimmied inside of one, looked up and cracked home a lovely curling shot into the top corner for the first double-strike of his career.

10 Michael Essien v Everton
17/04/06

Everton were dead and buried by the time Michael Essien picked up the ball 30 yards from goal. He rode two challenges going into the box, dropped his shoulder and fired an unstoppable shot into the roof of the net before running to the fans behind the goal to celebrate in style!

ShaunWrightPhillips

Word**Search**

Figure out what the clues represent. Then find the words in the grid.
Words can go horizontally, vertically or diagonally in all eight directions

```
R N P N A L I M C A L G N G T K
X K R O X L M Q K T G N Q N N I
D R N T R J O T H Y T R H E W S
N M M J P T Q O W L T K S R R O
D I F R R X U G P H L N K Q I R
T C C K K N B G G R H I M P G A
S H Y X H Q M I A O E R O G H J
A A N K C B E F J L T V K N T I
O E F L E Z Z D Z K W G I V P R
C L K N C B U T N E J C C L H I
Y E L F R G G B S Q W B T H I J
R S Q J T P Q T C C N K V T L L
O S T M E C H Q C E L E R Y L N
V I V D P A Y L T D M Z T L I H
I E Y T M S R E N O I S N E P M
P N F O O T B A L L I C O N S B
```

CLUES

Answers on
page 60/61

Czech Republic and Chelsea keeper
Shaun, who joined from Manchester City
Surname of Icelandic star who left for Barcelona
Favourite vegetable of Chelsea fans
Country of Jose Mourinho & Ricardo Carvalho
Club Joe Cole and Frank Lampard joined from?
Andriy Shevchenko's former club
Team the Blues played five times in 05/06

Country of Didier Drogba
Glasgow Celtic bought this player in 2006
Chelsea's Ghanaian midfielder
Number of points Chelsea won 2005/06 title by
Sky One TV series on Chelsea Academy
What kind of animal is Stamford the Chelsea mascot?
One of the Chelsea's nicknames – The…

Q&A WITH
NEIL BATH (NB)

1 - Where did the idea for Football Icon come from?
NB: A gentleman named Damien O'Brien is the 50/50 part-owner of Football Icon. He approached Chelsea's Group Business Affairs Director, Paul Smith, with the idea of running a TV programme where the winner wins a professional contract. Paul and Damian then spoke to various TV companies to gauge interest and at that stage I was approached to take the project forward and work out with my academy staff the way in which the competition would be structured.

2 - How many applicants did you have for the first series?
NB: We had 22000 calls and 6000 applicants!

Chelsea have again joined up with Sky One to produce Football Icon 2 – the reality TV series that offers the chance of a professional contract with the Blues. Head of Chelsea FC's Academy, Neil Bath (main pic), reveals the secrets behind the popular show:

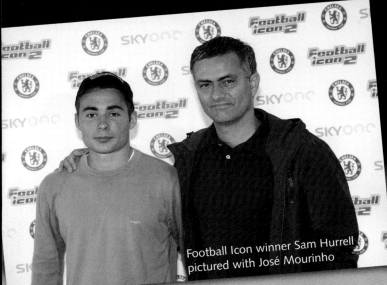

Football Icon winner Sam Hurrell pictured with José Mourinho

3 - How is Sam Hurrell progressing?
NB: Sam has made good progress and has had his contract extended for one more year.

4 - You took another lad on, Mark Gradosielski, as well - how did he get on last season?
NB: Mark is currently having trials at a number of clubs.

5 - Does the producer let you get on with things or ask you to make things more dramatic?
NB: No - I don't let the producer do anything other than how things are always handled at the academy. In other words, they film us doing our normal job and nothing more.

6 - How much involvement does José Mourinho have?
NB: José supports the project and is more involved as we get closer to making the final decision.

7 - Do you enjoy being involved or does it add a lot to your workload?
NB: I do enjoy being involved - initially it did take up a lot of my time but now we are a year down the line I anticipate myself not being so involved day-to-day.

8 - What do the other Chelsea Academy players make of it all?
NB: The lads understand the concept and are very professional and follow the programme on TV!

9 - Is it hard telling players you have to let them go?
NB: It is always difficult giving bad news to young players – giving bad news to the Icon lads is difficult, but nothing compared to telling players that you may have worked with for a number of years (i.e. regular academy players).

10 - Football Icon2 - has anything changed from the first series?
NB: We are always looking to improve so there are a number of changes, but the main one being the judges - last year it was myself and Ray Wilkins, however with Ray's involvement at Millwall we could not use him and have decided to add Eddie Newton and

Jamie Redknapp to the panel with myself as Chair.

11 - Is the interest greater because people know what it's all about now ?
NB: I am not involved in the recording of calls but I gather there is a lot more interest, particularly in the London area. I attended the London roadshow in Hammersmith and it looked great – lots of participants and fantastic organisation from the Icon staff.

12 - Do you think other clubs will follow Chelsea's lead?
NB: It will be difficult because we have got in first - our intention is to develop the project and possibly take it into other countries – watch this space – ha, ha!

chelseaFC 57

Andriy
Shevchenko

JohnTerry
DidierDrogba

QuizAnswers

ANSWERS TO BIG CHELSEA QUIZ (From page 20&21)

01 LASSANA DIARRA
02 HERNAN CRESPO
03 USA
04 LION
05 LEEDS UNITED
06 TWICE
07 GEREMI
08 HERNAN CRESPO – FLORIDA, ARGENTINA
09 GOALKEEPER
10 BRAZIL
11 TRUE
12 95
13 CRYSTAL PALACE, ARSENAL, WEST HAM, CELTIC, NOTTINGHAM FOREST, BURNLEY
14 COLCHESTER UNITED
15 NOTTINGHAM FOREST
16 CELTIC
17 LENNY PIDGELEY
18 SYLVAIN DISTIN
19 FALSE
20 1905
21 JOHN
22 STUART PEARCE (MANCHESTER CITY)
23 FRANK ARNESEN
24 REAL MADRID
25 JIMMY GREAVES (1958, 1959 & 1960)
26 BOBBY TAMBLING (202 GOALS BETWEEN 1958-70)
27 CLAUDIO RANIERI
28 PETER OSGOOD
29 DAMIEN DUFF
30 TRUE
31 BOLTON WANDERERS (5-1)
32 FIVE
33 PARMA
34 13
35 PETER KENYON
36 CLAUDE MAKELELE
37 JOHN TERRY, FRANK LAMPARD, WILLIAM GALLAS, JOE COLE
38 TWICE (2005, 2006)

WHO SAID THIS? (From page 22)

01 MIKEL JOHN OBI
02 MICHAEL BALLACK
03 ANDRIY SHEVCHENKO
04 SALOMON KALOU
05 CLAUDE MAKELELE
06 JOHN TERRY
07 ARJEN ROBBEN
08 DIDIER DROGBA
09 WILLIAM GALLAS
10 PETR CECH

SPOT THE BALL 1 (From page 27)

Answer H5

SPOT THE BALL 1 (From page 27)

Answer D2

WORD SEARCH (From page 55)

```
R N P N A L I M C A L G N G T K
X K R O X L M Q K T G N Q N N I
D R N T R J O T H Y T R H E W S
N M M J P T Q O W L T K S R R O
D I F R R X U G P H L N K Q I R
I C C K K N B G G R H I M P G A
T S H Y X H Q M I A O E R O H J
S A N K C B E F J L T V K N I I
O E L Z Z Z D Z K W G I V R I J
C L E N C B U T N E J C C L H L
Y L E F R G G B S Q W B T H I N
Q S L R T P O T C C N K V T L L
R Q J T M E C H Q C E L E R Y L L
O M E I V D P A Y L T D M Z T L I H
V I E Y T M S R E N O I S N E P M M B
P N F O O T B A L L I C O N S B
```

QUIZ DETECTIVE
(From page 39)

1 STEVE CLARKE

2 JOE COLE

3 HERNAN CRESPO AND PETR CECH

4 JOHN TERRY

5 CLAUDE MAKELELE

6 DAMIEN DUFF

7 MICHAEL BALLACK

8 SHEVCHENKO SIGNS

ANAGRAMS (From page 38)

01 MICHAEL ESSIEN

02 MICHAEL BALLACK

03 ANDRIY SHEVCHENKO

04 ASIER DEL HORNO

05 MIKEL JOHN OBI

06 SALOMON KALOU

07 LASSANA DIARRA

08 ANTHONY GRANT

09 YVES MAKALAMBAY

10 JOE COLE

CROSSWORD (From page 50)

FrankLampard**&**John**Terry**